bush
PUBLISHING
& associates

AMAZING LOVE

*A Revelation
of God's
Love for You*

BY SAMUEL MARTINEZ

All scripture quotations, unless otherwise noted, are from the *New King James Version*. Copyright © 1982 by Thomas Nelson Inc. Used by Permission. All rights reserved.

Scripture quotations marked AMP are taken from the *Amplified Bible*. Copyright © 1954, 1958, 1962, 1964, 1965, 1987 By the Lockman Foundation. Used by permission. (www.Lockman.org)

Scripture quotations marked NKJV are taken from the New King James Version®. Copyright © 1982 by Thomas Nelson. Used by permission. All rights reserved.

Copyright © 2015 Samuel Martinez

Amazing Love Ministries
216 S. Citrus St. P.O. BOX 503
West Covina Calif. 91791

Bush Publishing & Associates books may be ordered at www.BushPublishing.com or www.Amazon.com.
For further information, please contact:
Bush Publishing & Associates
www.BushPublishing.com

ISBN-13: 978-1-944566-00-5

All rights reserved. No part of this book shall be reproduced, stored in a retrieval system, or transmitted by any means, electronic, mechanical, photocopying, recording, or otherwise, without written permission from the publisher.

Table of Contents

Introduction: For Whom this Book Is Written 1
1 God Is Love 5
2 In the Beginning, Love 7
3 Our Great God and His Great Love 9
4 Christianity Versus Religion 11
5 Believe and Speak 13
6 The Width, Length, Depth and Height of His Love 15
7 Superabundant Love 17
8 That Your Joy May Be Full 19
9 The Apple of His Eye 21
10 I Am the Chosen 23
11 Before 25
12 We Have Seen, Looked Upon and Handled Love 27
13 Love and Fellowship 29
14 The Life 31
15 And Have Loved Them as You Have Loved Me 33

16 Great, Wonderful and Intense Love … 35

17 Give Us this Day Our Daily Bread … 37

18 The Battle Cry of the Believer, Part One … 39

19 The Battle Cry of the Believer, Part Two … 41

20 Sin Consciousness Versus Love Consciousness … 43

21 Great Is Thy Faithfulness … 45

22 Behold the Love … 47

23 But God, Who Is Rich in Mercy… … 49

24 Faith That Works by Love … 51

25 Holy of Holies … 53

26 His Tender Mercies … 55

27 Made Alive by Love … 57

28 Raised Up by Love … 59

29 Seated with Love … 61

30 Treat Others with Goodness … 63

31 Go and Love … 65

Epilogue … 67

Scriptures … 71

Appendix … 77

About the Author … 81

Introduction

FOR WHOM THIS BOOK IS WRITTEN

If you do not consider yourself a Christian and are reading this book, thank you for taking the time to read it. Most of what you have probably heard of the God of the Bible is not true. He does not steal, kill or destroy. He is the life-giver. The Bible calls Him love. He is good and His mercy endures forever. So if you do not consider yourself a Christian, this book is for you. Hopefully, it will give you an introduction to the real God of the Bible. Basically, if we want to know what God is like, all we have to do is look at Jesus. Without a doubt, the biggest obstacle to people knowing the real God of the Bible is Christians themselves. We have had many misconceptions about the God of the Bible ourselves. However, the Bible is very clear on the nature of God.

Therefore, if you do consider yourself a Christian, this book is also for you. Read this book a chapter a day with the Bible at your side. Read the scriptures given. Prove them out. The Bible plainly states that God is for us and is on our side. Scripture further states that every good and perfect gift is from Him. If it is good it is our God. If it is not good it cannot be God. Look at Jesus. He only did good. He fed the hungry and healed the sick. Then on top of this He gave His life. Romans 8:32 states that if God gave Jesus for us (the greatest gift He could give us) will He not freely give US all things? Matthew 7:11 states that if we as natural parents know and desire to give our children good things how MUCH MORE does God desire to give US good things. He loves you, my reader. So enter into the most wonderful study on earth—a study into the true nature of our Heavenly Father. He loves you.

Amazing

A Revelation

of God's

Love for You

1

GOD IS LOVE

Perhaps there is no simpler, and yet more profound, truth than this one—God loves you. Alongside this simple and yet profound truth is another one—God is love. The God of the Bible, the God and Father of our Lord Jesus Christ, is love.

The Bible teaches that God is love. It teaches that God loves you individually. The entire Bible was written to show mankind that the God of Abraham, Isaac and Jacob—the creator of the entire universe, loves you.

However, as simple as this truth is, none is perhaps more difficult for people, even Christians, to believe. Religions and religious regulations have been built around trying to get the approval of man-made deities. However, you can never earn the love of the true God—the God and Father of the Lord Jesus Christ. That is why He sent Jesus to earth. That is why Jesus died for you and why

Jesus lives to intercede for you. You can never earn His approval. It is a gift. He loves you.

Though He may not always approve of your actions, He loves you. Love is not love if it has to be earned. Love is not love if you have to do something to be worthy of it. The pressure is gone. The striving is gone. He loves you. Accept it. Believe it. Live by it. Rest in His love and let it change your thinking and your speech. If you have never made Jesus the Lord of your life just pray, "Lord Jesus, I believe You died for me and rose from the dead. I receive You as my Lord and Savior." You have been born again and are now His child. It really is that simple. Love (God) did all the work. The only thing left was that simple prayer. He loves you!

....

Confession

God loves me. I am the the love
child of a love God!

....

In the Beginning, Love

Since God is love and in the beginning there was God, then everything starts with love. In the beginning God (who is love) created the heavens and the earth (Genesis 1:1). Everything God has ever made or will ever make will be a result of His love. Every creative act in Genesis chapter 1 was due to His love for man that He was about to create. All things were made by love and without love was not anything made that was made (John 1:3).

Before we can ask and believe God for anything, we must believe that He loves us. It is impossible to have faith in someone that I am not convinced loves me. Before we can ask and believe God for healing, we must believe that He loves us and wants us well as we love our children and want them well. Before we can believe God for provision, we must believe that He loves us and desires, as any good father, that we live well. To not have a developed consciousness of God's love is to be sin conscious and be condemnation minded. Both hinder us from coming boldly to the throne of grace. So before beginning to believe God for healing, provision or anything, ask yourself the question, "Am I convinced that God loves me?" If not, spend time feeding yourself on the verses in the end of this book. Feed them into your spirit and begin to declare daily, "Thank you Father for loving me."

In the beginning was also the Word of love (John 1:1)— God's Word. And the Word (of love) was with God and the Word (of love) was God (John 1:1). God and His Word are one. The Word of God, the Bible, was written to reveal His love to us. That is why it is the Word of love. The Bible was not written to prove His existence but reveal His essence. The Lord is the essence of mercy and truth... Psalm 25:10 (Harrison translation). We must learn to read the Bible correctly. It is not a lengthy list of do's and don'ts. It is God speaking to us as a loving Father (who knows best) what to avoid and what to do in order to enjoy all the good He has provided for us. He loves you.

....

Confession

My Heavenly Father loves me.
He is the essence of mercy and love.
He desires only good for me.

....

3

OUR GREAT GOD AND HIS GREAT LOVE

Something that is very obvious to most people is the greatness of God. Anyone who could create the heavens and the earth by speaking them into existence is great beyond our natural mind's ability to comprehend. But let's consider this. The Bible does not major on God's great power but His great love, mercy and goodness. Of course God is great in power. However, think about this truth. He is great in power because of His great love.

I am pretty easy to get along with. I believe with God's help I can get along with everyone, even those who refuse to get along with me. Most people call me a pretty calm person. However, treat my wife or son wrongly and you will experience my power. If my wife and son are in danger, you will see my great power. In the case of my wife, I have a covenant with her. You may not see my great power when it comes to another person, but when it comes to her I am in covenant with her. As a Christian you have a covenant with God sealed in the blood of His Son whom He loves (Matthew 3:17, John 10:17, Hebrews 6:17).

Does God love you? Well by now, as you have been reading this little book, you are hopefully starting to become convinced that He does. Here is a correct statement—God loves you. Here is a truer statement—God greatly loves you. How about that? Everything God does He does it in a great and extravagant way. Look at the number of stars, fish, flowers and colors. If we had designed the earth we would have formed three kinds of fish, four different colors and three kinds of trees. What about 10 billion stars? Most of us would have stopped after a few thousand, but not God.

In Daniel 10:11 the angel said that Daniel was "greatly loved." Acts 10:34 states that God is no respecter of persons. If He greatly loved Daniel He greatly loves you. Receive this today.

···

Confession

I am greatly loved by my great God
and Savior. He greatly loves me.

···

CHRISTIANITY VERSUS RELIGION

Christianity is not a religion. Religion is a man-made set of rules formed to give some sort of assistance to a guilty conscience and to be accepted by a man-made deity. The key phrase is man-made. Christianity is not a man-made set of regulations and rules, although, in some areas it has been made into that. Christianity is God's plan to restore fellowship with fallen mankind. However, in order to fellowship with mankind, God had to die for man because the sin in mankind necessitated a payment that only a spotless Being could pay. Hence, Jesus the spotless Son of God entered earth.

Wasn't there any other way to pay for mankind's sin? No. Many have argued as to why God made man when He knew man would reject Him. The reason is simple—Love. God was willing to experience the rejection because of His love for man and because He already had a plan to restore man back into fellowship with Him. When man sinned he died spiritually and a Savior was now needed.

Why did God create man knowing eventually He was going to have to die for him? Love.

No, Christianity is not a set of rules and regulations. God loves you and wants you to know that in knowing His great love your conscience is purified. No more constant needing to rush to rituals, rules, etc. etc. to calm it. A license to sin, you ask? No, a license to have a dynamic relationship with Him.

A license to disobey? No, an empowerment to obey out of the recognition of our Father's love. In the Old Covenant we were commanded to love God with all our heart, soul and strength. No one ever could. In the New Covenant we are empowered to love Him because He first loved us (1 John 4:19).

··

Confession

Thank You Father for sending Jesus to die
for me and restore my relationship with You.
Thank You for loving me.

··

5

BELIEVE AND SPEAK

Faith is believing and speaking the Word of God (2 Corinthians 4:13). Faith is not just believing, but believing and speaking. Hence, if we say we believe that God loves us we must speak it. If we are not truly convinced that God loves us, it is even more important to speak what the word declares. Say it daily by faith, "Thank you Father for loving me. I receive your love." Declare as the apostle John stated, "I am the disciple that God loves." God is not a respecter of persons. The more I declare that I am loved, the more real it becomes in me and the more I believe it and speak it. Faith comes by hearing and hearing, so the more I hear myself saying it, the more faith comes and the more I obtain a revelation that God loves me. Don't wait to feel His love. Say it by faith and receive it by faith. "Thank You Father for loving me. I receive it in Jesus name." Never say that nobody loves you even when you feel that way. Don't plant that into your spirit. You are loved. Say it.

Confess that, as Jesus is in the bosom of the Father (John 1:18), so are you. Confess that Jesus loves you as much as the Father loves Him (John 15:9) and that the Father loves you as much as He loves Jesus (John 17:23). The more you confess the love of God the more it will grow in your heart. Then do not be surprised when one day as you are thanking the Father for loving you that you actually hear Him tell you, "Thank you, son (or daughter) for loving Me." What a way to live. He loves you!

Confession

Because I have the same Spirit of Faith I believe and say that I am loved. I am the disciple whom Jesus and the Father love.

6

THE WIDTH, LENGTH, DEPTH AND HEIGHT OF HIS LOVE

In Ephesians 3:16 the apostle Paul prays that we be strengthened with might by His Spirit in our inner man. He prayed this so that we would know what is the width, length, depth and height of His love (Ephesians 3:17-18). Well, ask yourself just how wide (width) is God's love? Well it is wide enough to embrace all races, colors of people, nationalities and ethnic groups. It is wide enough to embrace all socioeconomic groups and all people regardless of education, social achievements or physical appearances.

How long (length) is it? It is long enough to reach everyone. The Bible states in Jeremiah 31:3 that God loves us with an everlasting love and has drawn us to Himself with His love. How long is God's love? Long enough to reach everyone and draw them unto Him.

How deep (depth) is God's love? Deep enough to reach even the lowest sinner—people we would have a hard time loving or forgiving. In my case I was at the lowest place I had ever been in my life but His love reached me even at my lowest and set me at the highest place a born again believer can be placed—at the right hand of the Father in heavenly places (Ephesians 2:5). That is the height of His love. I went from the lowest to the highest. Thank you Jesus!

> *I've been seated with Jesus in heavenly places in Christ*
> *I've been seated with Jesus in heavenly places in Christ*
> *I've been given His power I've been given His name*
>   *Now in this life*
> *I rule and I reign*
> *'Cause I'm seated with Jesus In heavenly places in*
>   *Christ*
>
> © 1992/Faith Life Publications/Branson, MO

Now get this, if you have made Jesus your Lord and Savior you are seated at the right hand of the Father, at the right hand of Love Himself. What a God and what love!

....

Confession

I am seated with Jesus at the right hand of love Himself. He loves me.

....

7

SUPERABUNDANT LOVE

We must constantly remind ourselves daily of the great love God has for us. Ephesians 2:7 (Amplified version of the Bible) states that God intends to show through the ages to come His immeasurable, limitless and surpassing love to us. This is how much God loves us—in an immeasurable, limitless and surpassing way. The same Paul, in describing the love of God, uses the phrase in the Amplified Version (1 Timothy 1:14) "superabundant and beyond measure." Again, here is how much God loves us—in a superabundant and beyond measure manner. No wonder the psalmist stated in Psalm 107, "Oh that men would praise the Lord for His goodness and for His wonderful works to the children of men."

Let's thank God for His **immeasurable, limitless, surpassing love** and for His **superabundant** and **beyond measure love** for us. God's love is as immeasurable, limitless, surpassing, superabundant and beyond measure as He is. Expect to see the immeasurable, limitless, surpassing, superabundant and beyond measure love of God in your life every day. Expectation is the breeding ground for miracles. Manifestation begins with expectation. Believe the love and you will see the love. He loves you so expect to see His love manifested in your life today. What your mind may have a struggle understanding or receiving, your spirit will take in. Feed the following confession into your spirit daily.

....

Confession

My Father loves me in an immeasurable, limitless and surpassing manner. I am loved super abundantly and beyond measure.

....

8

THAT YOUR JOY MAY BE FULL

In John 16:23 and 24, Jesus mentions that the Father wants to answer our prayers so that our joy may be full. What a God! What a Father! He actually wants me happy and joyful. Religions paint a picture of deities that are only concerned about being worshipped and the need to be appeased. But our Father, our God, wants us to be enjoying life.

I have a sweet fellowship with my wife. In our relationship all I am is available to her and all she is also is available to me. The same exists in my relationship with God. All He is—is also available to me. He lives in me. I love Him. The greatest joy mankind can ever experience is in fellowship and the highest fellowship mankind can have is with its creator, our Heavenly Father.

John stated in 1 John 1:3 that he wrote to us so that we could have fellowship with one another and true fellowship with the Son and the Father. Then he adds in verse 4 of the first chapter, "These things we write that your joy may be full." Fellowship brings fullness of joy. Fellowship with God brings the greatest fullness of joy. Now get this GREAT truth. The greatest fellowship we can have with one another is around the great truth that He loves us. As we ALL grow in the revelation that He loves us our fellowship increases with the increase that only God can give.

Wow! He loves us. He loves you. Thank Him for loving you even when you do not feel loved and great joy will rise up inside you. He loves you. He wants you to have fullness of joy.

Confession

I have fellowship with my Father and Jesus today because They love me. I am walking in the fullness of joy because I am loved.

9

THE APPLE OF HIS EYE

Deuteronomy 32:10 AMP, He found him in a desert land, In the howling wasteland of a wilderness; He kept circling him, He took care of him, He protected him as the apple of His eye.

Psalm 17:8-9 NKJV, Keep me as the apple of your eye; hide me under the shadow of your wings, From the wicked who oppress me, From my deadly enemies who surround me.

Zechariah 2:8 NKJV, For thus says the Lord of Hosts: "He sent Me after glory, to the nations which plunder you; for he who touches you touches the apple of His eye."

The phrase "apple of the eye" is a phrase that suggests something is very precious. In "The Dictionary of Cliches" by James Robers (Ballantine Books, New York, 1985), he mentions that in old English the eye's pupil was known as the apple because the pupil was thought to be spherical. Presumably because the apple was the most common spherical object around, the phrase developed. Due to sight being such a precious thing, the phrase has come to be applied for something that is very dear and precious.

In the verses noted above we see that the Lord has promised to encircle, instruct, keep and hide us. All these Words speak of His care and protection for us. The verse in Zechariah indicates that God notices when we are wronged as God took notice on how Egypt and Pharaoh were treating Israel. Be encouraged! God notices when we are wrongly treated and will act on our behalf. More than wanting judgment on those who mistreat us, this should encourage us to maintain a godly and loving attitude in the midst of being wronged. God will bless us when we love those who mistreat us. God will bless us because we are the apple of His eye, because we are very precious to Him. We are His most prized possession.

....

Confession

He loves me. I am the apple of God's eye,
His most prized possession.

....

10

I Am the Chosen

I generally enjoy going shopping with my wife. When purchasing a dress she follows a regular routine. She will go to one store after another until she finds the dress she decides to buy. In spite of enjoying the experience of shopping with her I have to admit that the first dress that she tries on is generally good enough for me. So I tell her to buy it and let's go home. Ah, but no, she will go through several more stores until she finally decides on one. That dress is now the chosen one. It was hand-picked by her. It is the same with you. God hand-picked you. Ephesians 1:5 states that we were chosen, hand-picked before the foundation of the world.

I really like avocados but rarely purchase the first one I see at the store. I take my time and find the chosen one. You are God's chosen one, chosen for a divine purpose before the foundation of the world. God picked you out before you were even born and took time to plan a glorious life for you. Both the prophet Jeremiah and the apostle Paul point this out. You are probably thinking, "But Samuel, He chose everyone before the foundation of the world. He hand- picked all of us." Yes! Isn't that great! What a God and what love! He loves you. You are God's **chosen**. Receive it and declare it. You will obtain a revelation of this the more you say it.

Confession

I am God's Chosen. He chose me before the foundation of the world. He knew me before the foundation of the world. He loves me! There is a divine plan and purpose on my life.

11

BEFORE

John 1:1 states that in the beginning was the Word and the Word was with God and the Word was God. That which was from the beginning is love because God is love. Love has always been here. There has never been a time that God has not been so, there has never been a time that love has not been. Therefore, love has always been here and love will always be here. Because love has always been it will always be. Before earth existed love was and love is. Before the stars, the planets, the rivers and the valleys, love was and love will always be.

Before even I was, love was and is. Before you were created; before you came to earth love was already here. Love planned everything. Love planned your birth, your coming to earth and love planned out every detail of your life before you were even born. No, you are not a puppet in God's hands. He lets us decide whether we will walk in the good life He has planned for us.

When you arrived love was here. That which was from the beginning will be here with you for all eternity since God is love and God is eternal. This is why in the Bible many times God (love) states, "I will never leave you nor forsake you." He loves you.

> Before the light of the morning
> God (love) is there, God is there
> Before the rooster blows its horn in the morning
> God is there, God is there
> Before the morning cry of the newborn
> Before the birds sing their symphony
> In the morning
> Before the dew appears in the morning
> God (love) is already there.
> (Song, © 2012, Samuel Martinez)

No wonder the psalmist stated, "Where can I flee from Your presence?" The answer is nowhere. Wherever you go, He is already there. Love is there already, ready to continue to love you. Receive His love. He loves you.

• •

CONFESSION

Thank You Father that I have always been
and will always be loved by You.
I am eternally loved.

• •

12

WE HAVE SEEN, LOOKED UPON AND HANDLED LOVE

In 1 John 1:2, John states that he heard, saw, looked upon and handled the Word of life. He was talking about Jesus. He heard, saw and looked upon Him the Word of life. Jesus was and is the express image of the Father. To see Jesus is to see God, the Father, Who is love. So John heard love. He looked upon it and handled it.

John is excited because he heard love, he saw love in action, and he handled it. By handling it he meant that he saw how love operated in the life of Jesus and he put it in action in his own life. He had experiential knowledge of it. Now he wants to declare it to others. When you have heard love speak, when you have looked upon it and have handled it, you want to share it with others.

Read the Word of God, the Bible. In His book you will hear His love, see it, look upon it and handle it. See how it works, how it changes people. Do not read the Book with preconceived ideas. The Bible was written to make God's love known so we could hear it, look upon it, and see it in action. As you read the Bible (particularly the New Testament) read it with the thought that you will hear love, see love and observe it in action. God loves you. He wants you to know Him intimately. He is right in the Bible revealing Himself to you. Read slowly and you will hear love (God) speaking to you. You will hear love talk with you and say, "I love you and what I did for the person in the story you just read I want to do for you."

Declare this out loud before you read the word. "Father as I approach the Word I believe that I will encounter and experience Your love and see it today in a way I've never seen it before." He loves you!

Confession

Every day I am encountering the love of God in a fresh way. He loves me.

13

LOVE AND FELLOWSHIP

In 1 John 1:3, John states that his purpose in writing was so that all could have fellowship with the Father and His Son, Jesus. Mankind yearns for fellowship. We can call it bonding or a sense of belonging but it comes down to the same thing—fellowship. Mankind hungers for it—to feel the warmth of others, to sense the concern of others, to believe that we are valuable to others. We also need to believe that we can give all this to others as well. We thirst for the sharing of our lives with others. The intermingling of our lives with one another is necessary to our growth and development.

John stated, however, that only in love, who is God (and the concern for the needs of others more than our own) can true fellowship occur. Without love, relationships become abusive and self-centered where the root is selfishness. Only in love (the God-kind of love) is there true fellowship and only in love is there true growth.

John makes a tremendous statement that we can have fellowship with one another and more importantly with God, Himself, who is love. What joy this brings. The need to have fellowship with God has spawned all the religions in the world. The need to appease Him, and the need to have His approval. However, we do not have to appease Him (the true God) to have His approval when He already loves us just as we are.

Christianity is not a religion. In its simplest form it is having fellowship with the Father. It is God wanting to have fellowship with mankind. The problem was that mankind was in sin and could not fellowship with a holy God. However, God had the answer. He sent His Son born of a woman to pay for mankind's sins. Now all we have to do is receive the gift of Jesus and fellowship is restored. Mankind created the division. God destroyed it in Jesus. To anyone who receives Jesus, fellowship is restored. Now talk to Him and have fellowship with Him every day. Share your life with Him. He loves you!

······································

Confession

Today I can have fellowship with my Heavenly Father—fellowship with Love Himself.

······································

14

THE LIFE

In 1 John 1:2, John stated that **the** life was manifested. Love (who is God) is life. Apart from love we only exist but we do not live. Apart from love our relationships die. Apart from love our ambitions and dreams are meaningless. What good are goals and dreams if once we reach them we cannot share them with others and for their benefit?

On the other hand, love gives life to our relationships. The home becomes alive when love is there. The worker bored with his menial tasks comes alive when he recognizes that instead of going to work to just do a job, he is going to be a blessing to others. His menial tasks, as boring as they may be, are needed by someone even if no one ever recognizes him for his mundane work. From the assembly line worker to the dishwasher, to the doctor, lawyer or teacher, we all work to enhance the life of others. At the least, we should see it that way.

The parent frustrated with the day-to-day tasks needs to realize that even menial tasks are serving love to others. Even if nothing is acknowledged our tasks need to be seen as blessing others. Our jobs and mundane tasks come alive. I become alive because of instead of looking to be blessed I now look for opportunities to bless others. Instead of looking for what others can do for me I am looking to what I can do for others. I come alive in love (who is God). I come alive with His life. I am now acting like Him. This truly honors our Father when we act like Him.

Confession

Today I walk in the love of God. I will walk like Him and honor Him.

And Have Loved Them as You Have Loved Me

John 17:23 is an awesome and almost too-good-to-be-true verse in the Bible. In it Jesus makes the awesome statement that the Father loves me as much as He loves Jesus. Just when I am becoming convinced that God really, really loves me, I run across this verse that God not only loves me, but that He loves me as much as He loves Jesus.

I have begun to understand that God loves me as much as He loves Jesus. But here is an issue. I've sinned. Jesus never sinned. I've disobeyed God and so have you. Jesus, however, never disobeyed. Jesus obeyed the Father perfectly even to the point of death on the cross. There has never been anyone who so perfectly pleased the Father as Jesus did.

Jesus never lied. Never had an unholy thought. Never displayed a wrong attitude. He was never resentful. He was never self-seeking. He was never proudful. Jesus never took account of wrongs done to Him. So it is not easy for many people to accept that God loves them as much as He loves Jesus.

But wait! I see it now. The instant I received Jesus as my Lord and Savior, God recreated me in Christ Jesus and placed me in Him. I am now in Him—the Beloved (Ephesians 1:6). I am the body of the Beloved. God has to love me as much as He loves Jesus because I am in Jesus and am one with Him. You cannot separate Jesus from His body, the Church.

When God sees me He sees Jesus. When He sees Jesus He sees me. He loves you as much as He loves Jesus! Say the following confession loud enough to hear yourself. Your mind will fight it but your spirit will give a great YES!

* * *

Confession

Thank You Father for loving me
as much as You love Jesus.

* * *

16

GREAT, WONDERFUL AND INTENSE LOVE

I suppose we have barely scratched the surface when it comes to having a full revelation of the love of God. In Ephesians 2:4 the apostle talks about God "who is rich in mercy." The Greek word for rich in this verse is 'plusios.' It means filthy rich. From this word plusios comes our English word plutocrat or someone who uses his wealth to influence others. Think of this. God uses His mercy (the riches of His mercy) to influence us. Most people have an idea of God using His power or even His judgments to influence us. The Amplified Bible in Ephesians 2:4 states, "But God—so rich is He in His mercy because of and in order to satisfy the **great** and **wonderful** and **intense** love with which He loved us..." Wow! God is intense in His love for us. Actually God is intense in everything He does. He never does anything half way so why would He love us in any other way?

Now let's deal with the word **wonderful.** God's love is full of wonder. It is awe-inspiring. What about the word **great**? Well God loves us greatly. The dictionary defines great as above the average in magnitude, intensity and importance. That sounds just like the love God has for us. Let me add more on the word intense. When I think of **intense,** I think of doing something with all we have. God is intense in His love for us. He loves us with every fiber of His being.

But the Amplified Version adds that God, in order to satisfy the great, wonderful and intense love He had for us, loved us even when we were dead and separated from Him. He then gave us His life. He reached out to us. It is almost as if God could not stand being separated from His love-created beings. No wonder the song of old calls it Amazing Grace.

Confession

Today God loves me in a great, wonderful and intense way. I am greatly, wondrously and intensely loved.

Give Us this Day Our Daily Bread—Grace, Mercy and Peace

Often we think of bread as physical provision and rightly so. Our Father is interested in our physical sustenance. He provided for His people daily in the wilderness. However, if physical sustenance is needed on a daily basis, how much more the spiritual sustenance of receiving God's love daily. So many times in his letters the apostle Paul began his letters by speaking grace and peace over those he was writing to. In 1 Timothy 1:2, he adds the word mercy. If you are like me, you have read quickly over the salutations to get into the meat of the letters. But some time back the Spirit of the Lord stopped me in the salutation and had me receive His grace, mercy and peace as a daily provision.

Grace—The unmerited, undeserved and unearned favor of God.

Mercy—His unconditional love that makes me more than a conqueror.

Peace—Calm in the midst of whatever is going on around me resulting in nothing missing and nothing broken because my Father loves me.

You have daily what you need from your Father. He planned for us before the foundation of the world and before we were sent to earth. But by the same token He plans and provides for us every day. Receive daily from His unlimited supply of grace, mercy and peace. He loves you!

....

Confession

Father, today I receive Your grace, mercy
and peace. Nothing can overcome me today
because I have received my daily provision
of Your grace, mercy an peace. I will let these
three govern me today.

....

The Battle Cry of the Believer, Part One

We all know the story of Jehoshaphat and the great armies that came against him (2 Chronicles chapter 20). He went to God and stated that he did not know what to do. I have often stated that Jehoshaphat did know what to do—turn to the God that loved him in the midst of a storm—in the midst of not knowing what to do in the natural.

As the story progresses, the Lord speaks to a prophet who tells the people a word from the Lord. The word was that they would not need to fight in the battle because, "The battle belongs to the Lord." So many times, I believe, we misuse this phrase and thus do nothing. Jehoshaphat knew that he had a part in releasing the mighty hand of God to fight for him. Jehoshaphat could have taken the word from the Lord and done nothing. He must have been impressed by the Spirit of God to do something to release the mighty hand of God. He put singers ahead of his army singing that God's mercy endures forever. This action released the mighty power of God that caused the attacking armies to destroy themselves. That is why I like to refer to the phrase, "The Lord is good and His mercy endures forever," as the battle cry of the believer. When attacked by the devil, may the first thing that comes out of our mouths be, "The Lord is good and His mercy endures forever." You will release the mighty hand of God in your midst. Sing it (the army of Jehoshaphat did) and say it,

The Lord is good and His mercy endures forever!

This phrase not only releases the power of God in our lives but helps us to focus our thoughts on the Lord and away from the negative thoughts that always come when the devil attacks. This phrase also prevents me from feeling sorry for myself or blaming God. I am then able to focus my mind on the God that loves me, thus putting me in a position to receive His wisdom. This is what Jehoshaphat did. Praise the Lord! He won and I can win, too!

· ·

Confession

The Lord is good and His mercy endures forever. He loves me. I win!

· ·

THE BATTLE CRY OF THE BELIEVER, PART TWO

To continue with yesterday's thought, every day we need to confess that the Lord is good and His mercy endures forever. Four things will happen the more we say this:

1. The more we will live expecting to see the goodness of God in our lives. As we have said before, expectation is the breeding ground for miracles.

2. The more our faith will grow in His love for us since faith comes by hearing and hearing (Romans 10:17).

3. The more God will manifest His love and goodness toward us. This is what good parents will do when their children praise them from a pure heart.

4. The less we will focus on what is not right in our lives thus preventing us from becoming negative and feeling sorry for ourselves.

Truly the Lord has been good to us and His mercy endures forever. So many times we lose focus on what the Lord has done for us already. Even when things occur that are unpleasant, there is always something to thank God for. The psalmist said, "Blessed are the people that know the joyful sound" (Psalm 89:15). We could say it this way. Blessed are the people that in the midst of difficulties still say, "The Lord is good and His mercy endures forever." Say it throughout the day and see if these four things will not manifest in your life.

I have said many times that this statement that the Lord is good and His mercy endures forever is the foundation of the Bible. Let it become the foundation of your life as well. The psalmist further stated that he would have fainted unless he would have believed to see the goodness of the Lord (Psalms 27:13). Believe to see it today. He loves you.

· ·

Confession

The Lord is good and His mercy endures forever. I am expecting to see His goodness and mercy in my life today. He loves me.

· ·

20

SIN CONSCIOUSNESS VERSUS LOVE CONSCIOUSNESS

Hebrews 10:2 states that the Jews had a sin consciousness because the sacrifices they offered year after year could not cleanse them from their sins. It only covered their sins. Sin consciousness is not just feeling guilty when I sin, but walking around 24 hours a day seeing myself as a sinner. That is, thinking of myself as a sinner and talking of myself as being "only a sinner saved by grace."

But since Jesus came, our sins past, present and future have been remitted. This word means removed. They no longer exist and more than that our sin nature has been removed. I am no longer a sinner by nature, though, at times, I do miss it. The reason the devil reminds me of past sins is not just so that I will feel guilty (this is bad enough) but so that I will still see myself as a sinner. But my nature has changed. In this same chapter in Hebrews, Paul mentions that now that we have received Jesus as our Lord and Savior, God remembers our sins no more. He now sees you in Christ— the righteousness of God in Him. We were washed by the blood and now God sees us in our new nature.

Now replace sin consciousness with love consciousness. Every time Satan reminds you of your sins remind him you are loved. Every time he reminds you of past failures stop and say with your mouth, "I am loved, God loves me. I am no longer a sinner. My nature has changed. I have the love nature inside of me. He loves me." Replace sin consciousness with love consciousness. He loves you and for that reason He has wiped away all your sin and given you a new nature—His nature which is love. Your nature has changed.

2 Corinthians 5:21 states that we have been made the righteousness of God in Christ. Now change your talk and thoughts about you and let that love consciousness and righteousness consciousness dominate you. He loves you!

··

Confession

I am free from sin consciousness since I am the righteousness of God in Christ. He loves me! I will walk today in love and righteousness consciousness.

··

21

GREAT IS THY FAITHFULNESS

Remember the old classic song "Great is Thy Faithfulness"? Yes, God is faithful, but faithful to what? He is faithful to His Word, of course. However, just as relevant is what is found in Lamentations 2:22 where mention is made that the faithfulness of God is great. The writer of Lamentations goes on to add that His mercies are new every morning. His love is never stale or worn out. His mercies are fresh every morning. So we can state that great is the faithfulness of God in showing us His mercies new every morning. Every morning, without exception, God wants to show us His love in a way we have never seen. He is faithful to that. He is faithful to be merciful and loving.

Get up in the morning confessing this: "I thank you Father that You are a good God Who gives good things (Matthew 7:11). Therefore, good things are coming to my life today. I expect today to see Your love in a way I have never seen before."

God is faithful to love you every day and show you His love in a way you have never seen before. This is what eternity with our Father will be like—God showing us every day His compassions in a way we have never seen before. But why wait until eternity? We are already in it. Expect to see His great love, His mercies and His compassions every day in a way you have never seen before and you will. Even when negative things happen in our day don't quit expecting to see His love. He loves you.

Be expecting today. Everything starts with expectation. Expect and you will see. Live today all the day expecting to see His love in manifestation. He loves you!

Confession

I will see the love of God today in a way I have never seen before because His mercies are new every morning.

Behold the Love

Recently in my time with the Lord I was meditating 1 John 3:1. I began to praise the Lord for His goodness. After a few minutes something I had to attend to that day came into my mind and I started to worry. I caught myself and stopped the worry thoughts and realized I needed to get back to the verse and meditate, think about my Father's love.

Isn't that what we have to do every day and sometimes throughout the day—stop ourselves and on purpose think about His love? When tempted to worry or after having yielded to worry, run back to 1 John 3:1 and behold the love. Even when persecution comes or someone does not treat you in a way that they should have, run to 1 John 3:1 to behold the love. Here are a few synonyms to the word behold— see, contemplate, think, visualize, meditate and my favorite having grown up in the 60's—check it out.

In the Word of God we behold, we see the love. We also behold or see it in Christ. Run to Him when the pressures of life come. In Christ, God has shown how much He loves you. See how much He has done for you. Think about it. Meditate about it. Contemplate it. Check it out. Read Isaiah chapter 53 slowly. Behold the love. He loves you. Everything Christ did on earth and is now doing in heaven is for us. See and embrace the love. Behold the love. Never for one moment think that you have no control over your thoughts. When you open your mouth to declare that you are loved the negative thoughts break up. You have the spirit of power, love and self control inside of you (2 Timothy 1:7). Behold the love!

Confession

Father, by faith I behold Your love. I declare that today I will hold it in my mind, speaking it out of my mouth. Thank You for loving me.

But God, Who Is Rich in Mercy...

Ephesians 2:1 states that we were dead in trespasses and sins. Verse 4 of the same chapter, however, adds the words BUT GOD who is rich in mercy. The two words 'BUT GOD' are so rich in meaning. We were dead in sin which was our nature—children of wrath. BUT GOD is so rich in mercy. Where would we be without those two words? I was lost— BUT GOD. I was separated from Him for all eternity—BUT GOD. You may be in a seemingly impossible situation. Most everybody has at one time or another. Think of this. We were spiritually dead. I can't think of any situation more impossible or difficult than that. Dead not physically but worse, spiritually.

Our inner nature, our spirit, was dead and there was nothing we could do to get us out of the mess Adam thrust all mankind into. In fact, the Bible mentions that salvation was and is by grace because there was nothing we could do to get out of the mess.

Lost, dead and doomed. BUT GOD. Thank God for those two words. If you are facing an insurmountable circumstance remember—BUT GOD. He got us out of the most insurmountable circumstance we can think of. He can and will get us out again. Stand on His Word. Stand on the fact that He loves you. The Word states He does. Trust His love. BUT GOD. Those two words mean He refused to leave mankind in the situation we had gotten ourselves into.

You may even feel the mess you are in now is your own fault. Therefore, you think you have to get yourself out of it by your own efforts. Do not shut off His mercy. Remember that He did not have to get involved when we were dead— He chose to. Let Him help now. He loves you. He does not desire you to stay where you are. BUT GOD. His mercy endures forever.

· ·

Confession

Father, I thank You that You did not leave
me in the condition I was in before I
met you and you will not leave me
in the situation I am in now.

· ·

Faith That Works by Love

Galatians 5:6 states that our faith works by love. Hebrews 11:6 shows that it is impossible to please God without it. God wants us to believe and have faith in His love. 1 John 4:16 states that we have known and believed the love God has for us. If you are standing in faith in some area, nothing will boost your faith more than the knowledge that He loves you. Are you standing in faith for your healing, the salvation of a loved one or some financial need? Then remember that He loves you. Through faith and patience you will see the victory. Keep speaking the Word. He is on your side. The Bible states that God is **for** us, He is **in** us and He is **with** us. So when you are speaking the Word also state this, "My faith is working. My confession is working. The Word is working because He loves me. I will see the results of my standing in faith because He loves me."

Faith works by love means that I must walk in love with others for my faith to work. However, it also means that in order for my faith to work by love I must have confidence in His love for me. Again, let me state that He is for you (Rom. 8:31) and He is on your side (Psalm 118:6). Believe that as you stand in faith He is encouraging you to not let go of your faith. Let your faith work by the revelation that He loves you. He is not the one hindering the manifestation of what you are believing for. He is encouraging you not to quit because He loves you.

••••••••••••••••••••••••••••••••••••••

Confession

My faith is working because I walk in love and have faith in His love for me.

••••••••••••••••••••••••••••••••••••••

HOLY OF HOLIES

Hebrews 4:16 states to come boldly to the throne of Grace. Similar to this verse is Hebrews 10:19 that states that we have liberty to enter the Holy of Holies. If you are not familiar with Old Testament worship and the sacrifices of the Jewish nation, the Holy of Holies was the place that only the High Priest could enter, and only once a year. It was the holiest place in the Jewish temple, hence, the name. The way that the High Priest could enter the Holy of Holies was complex. Along comes Paul preaching Righteousness and states that we have boldness to enter by the blood of Jesus. Before the Old Testament priest could enter he had to make meticulous preparations (see Leviticus chapter 16). Additionally, he could only enter except by the shed blood of animals.

The Holy of Holies was where the very presence of God was. If the High Priest did not follow the prescribed rules as far as entering the Holy of Holies he would die. I have said all this to show what a statement Paul was making that WE could enter the Holy of Holies. As I was reading this verse one day I was impressed that the Holy of Holies in New Testament worship is the most intimate place that we can enter into. It is the very HEART of the Father God who is love. The Holy of Holies is the place that the Father wants us to enter—His very heart. The Holy of Holies is the heart of YOUR Father. Enter into the most intimate heart- warming time that you can have with the Father. The Holy of Holies is Communion with Love. Come on in, He says, and stay as long as you want. He loves you. You enter the Holy of Holies by the blood of Jesus and the recognition that He loves you. Believe and receive His love. You have a standing invitation to enter. He loves you.

··

Confession

Today I enter the Holy of Holies—the very
Heart of my Father. He loves me!

··

26

HIS TENDER MERCIES

Psalm 145:9 states that God's tender mercies are over all His works. His tender mercies are over you today. Have you ever felt that a cloud of doom and gloom was over you? Well, my friend, God did not put it there. He put His tender mercies over you, but many times our negative thoughts push those mercies away from us. He never stops loving us, but our thoughts do not allow that love over us to reign supreme in our lives. Since God is love we have to say that He has placed Himself over us. Remember the cloud by day and the fire by night in the Old Testament that protected and guided the people of God in the wilderness? Well, now it is His love that is over us. His love is over us guiding us and protecting us. Remember that Song of Solomon 2:2 states that His banner over us is love. He is over us expressing His ownership of us and His tender care.

Psalms 145:9 further states that His tender mercies are over all His works: not some of them, but all of them.

Your mistakes or past cannot stop the mercies from being over you unless you allow it. You may think God loves so and so because they are so good or go to church or whatever, but God loves you too even if you do not do all the things your friend does. Let me state this again. His tender mercies are over **all** His works. That includes you, my friend. No matter how you feel, step out in faith and receive this. Say it out loud, "The tender mercies of God are over me today!" Amen!

•••

Confession

> The tender mercies of God are over me today to guide and protect me. His banner over me is love. He cares for me tenderly.

•••

MADE ALIVE BY LOVE

I recently heard this in my spirit—I have been made alive by Love. Ephesians 2:1 states that we were made alive when we made Jesus the Lord and Savior of our lives. You and I were made alive by Love because God is Love. I was dead not only in sin but separated from God living in selfishness, self-centeredness and pride. But now I have been made alive in Love—in God who is Love. Do you remember Acts 19:20, that in Him we live and move and have our being? It is in Love that we live and move and have our being. It is in Love that we really live!

Yes, I was dead. I was separated from God who is Love. Separated from what gave life to my being, meaning to my existence and joy unspeakable and full of glory. I have been made alive by Love. I am now alive unto Love—alive unto God. I can now know Him, fellowship with Him and practice His presence every minute of the day. I can now hear His voice. I was dead to His voice but now I can hear His voice—the voice of Love. I am alive unto God. I am alive unto doing for others—putting others' needs above my own. I can know Him. In fact, I do know Him. I know Love. I have been made alive by Love. I now know Love because He (Love) lives in me. He walks with me and tells me that I am His own.

I am dead no more. I am imprisoned no more. He loves me. Love made me alive. I now live because I love. I was made alive by Love. Hallelujah. He gave me life when I was dead. What a gift. What a Savior. What a redemption! Praise the Lord!

••••••••••••••••••••••••••••••••••••••

Confession

I have been made alive by love. I live because Love (God) is in me. He loves me.

••••••••••••••••••••••••••••••••••••••

28

RAISED UP BY LOVE

Ephesians 2:6 states that God (Love) raised me from the dead. I was raised by Love. I was not only made alive by Love, but raised up by Love. Love raised me above the world's way of living to another realm—raised with Him.

Yes, He (Love) raised me from the dead—raised up by Love. Love raises me above the worldly way of living which includes condemnation, guilt, self-centeredness and fear. Love raised me. I am no longer in a lowly realm. I have been raised to the realm of Love. How I love the song we used to sing in my childhood—"Love Lifted Me."

> Love lifted me, Love lifted me
> When nothing else could help
> Love lifted me
> Love lifted me, Love lifted me
> When nothing else could help
> Love lifted me.

Yes, Love lifted me. 1 Samuel 12:8 states that God lifts the poor from the dust and lifts the beggar from the ash heap setting him among princes and thrones of glory. Let Love (God Himself) lift you today. Let this reality lift you today—God loves me. YOU ARE SOMEBODY. You are a love child of a love God. Let this raise you up, that you are important to God—to Love. In the 12th chapter of the book of Luke Jesus stated that God feeds the birds and then asks the question, "Are you not worth much more than they?" Of course we are. Let Love lift your inner picture of yourself. Let Love be the lifter of your head. The psalmist stated that God is the shield, glory and the lifter of my head (Psalms 3:3). Lift your head up. You are loved!

···

Confession

I have been raised up by love.
I no longer walk in guilt, condemnation,
selfishness or fear. He loves me!

···

29

SEATED WITH LOVE

Ephesians 2:7 states that I was also seated with Christ. He seated me where I am seated. I did not seat myself there so do not get upset when I tell you where I am seated. I have joint seating with Christ, with God, with Love Himself. In the natural joint seating brings certain privileges. In the spirit realm joint seating equates with the sharing of authority and power. Love seated me where I am seated so it is natural to assume that as I walk in Love (who is God) only then can I exercise my privileges from joint seating.

I am firmly seated where I am. Yes, I have authority and power. Let's use them. However, Ephesians 2:7 states **why** I was seated. I was seated so that in the ages to come He might show the exceeding riches of His grace to us through His beloved son Jesus. We have mentioned this before but I should add that the ages to come are not out in eternity somewhere when we all get to heaven. Eternity is life with Him. Eternal life, the life of God (Zoe life) began when you were born again. So we were seated with Him so that in the ages to come, so that in forever time if you will, so that in eternity, He might show off the exceeding riches of His everlasting Love. This is something to get excited about. God wants to make a show and He will. It has already started. We are in it. In fact we are the show. We are the benefactors of that show. That is why I was seated where I am. Hey, let's sit down and enjoy the show. He loves you. Expect to see today the exceeding riches of His love—grace in your life. Sit down. Stop toiling and receive His love.

Confession

I am expecting today to see the exceeding riches of His grace in my life. He loves me!

30

TREAT OTHERS WITH GOODNESS

For years I have had this statement as part of my regular vocabulary, that the Lord is good and His mercy endures forever. One day as I was meditating this verse I heard in my spirit the Lord saying, "Confess every day that the Lord is good and His mercy endures forever. Live every day like the Lord is good and His mercy endures forever and treat everyone like the Lord is good and His mercy endures forever." It is the last phrase that grabbed me. If we truly believe that the Lord is good and His mercy endures forever then we will treat people this way. Now that you are becoming fully persuaded that the Lord is good and that His mercy endures forever, go out and treat others like the Lord is good and His mercy endures forever.

After a time of prayer I recently heard God tell me about the people I pastor, "Teach them to know, teach them to grow and then teach them to go." Now that you know the love of the Father and are growing in it, go and tell others that God loves them and that He is not angry at them. Tell them that He is for them. Tell them that He is good and His mercy endures forever. Remember that we are the carriers of that love. People will not know unless you specifically tell them that He loves them. What a privilege we have to tell others of the love of our Father. Go now in Jesus' name.

Confession

I am a carrier of the love of God.
I am a minister of His grace.
I will tell others of my Father's love for them.

GO AND LOVE

1 John 3:1—Behold what manner of love the Father has bestowed upon us that we should be called the sons of God.

This is a very powerful verse. "What manner of love," says the King James Version. Another translation uses the word wonderful to describe the love (wonderful love). Wonderful means of course full of wonder and awe. It implies something that has the capacity to take your breath away. This is God's love; it leaves us breathless.

A couple of Spanish translations, however, use the word great in front of the word love. They state literally, "Look at the **great** love God has given us." God, our Father, does everything in great proportions. Look at the vastness of the universe. Nothing is small with God although in His greatness He leaves nothing unattended to in our lives, even the smallest need or desire.

God loves you but, He not only loves you He **greatly** loves you. We could paraphrase 1 John 3:1 to say think, ponder, meditate and contemplate the great love the Father has given unto us by making us His sons. The greatest thing the great God has done is make us His sons. Now all He has is mine. I now carry His nature, His love and His life. I am greatly loved.

Now, as we conclude this small book, go and love as He loves. You can do it. Peter uses the word fervent to describe the love we can show the world (1 Peter 4:7). Another translation uses the words 'intense' and 'unfailing' to show the love we can show the world (Amplified Version). We have already run across the word 'intense' in discovering that this is the way God loves us—intensely. We can then love fervently and intensely as He loves us. The world has never seen the love Christians are capable of showing one another, or the world. However, God is raising up an army of people who will show the world and others love as they have never seen before—a group of people fully convinced of how much God loves them and going out to the world loving others as they are loved. Go and love! He loves you—and the world.

Confession

My heavenly Father, the Great God,
loves me greatly. I am greatly loved;
therefore, I can greatly love.

EPILOGUE

Epilogue

I had finished writing this book when I was impressed to add a few additional thoughts. Read the Bible, my friend, on a daily basis. You can use this book to discover His love but nothing exceeds time in the Word and fellowship with Him.

Another thought I had was concerning those who are familiar with the Old Testament. You must remember that Jesus had not yet come to satisfy the claims of justice. Additionally, many times in the Old Testament when we see God sending judgment or a calamity to the wicked, the verbs are in the permissive tense. When we translate them into the English, the English having no permissive tense, the verses seem to point to God being the author of evil. But just think of this for a minute. If I mistreat my body God does not have to send judgment into my body in the way of a heart attack. Judgment is already built into the mistreatment of my body.

Well, let us keep it simple. Jesus stated if you have seen Me you have seen the Father. Did Jesus ever put evil, calamity or sickness on anyone? No, He did not. He removed those things. Jesus has satisfied the claims of justice. God is NOT holding our sins against us or the world. What a shame to go to hell which was NOT created for any man, when all our sins have been paid for. Remember John 10:10. It helps rightly divide the Word of God. If it steals, kills or destroys it is the devil. God only gives life. Job could not read his own book to understand that God was not the cause of his calamities as is stated in Job 3:25. Hey, remember that He loves you. He is on your side. I call you Blessed, my reader.

SCRIPTURES

Verses on God's Amazing Love

Psalm 25:10, The Lord is the essence of mercy and truth (Harrison Translation).

Psalm 118:1, Oh, Give thanks to the Lord for He is good! For His mercy endures forever.

Jeremiah 31:3, The Lord has appeared of old to me, saying: "Yes, I have loved you with an everlasting love; Therefore with lovingkindness I have drawn you."

John 15:9, As the Father loved Me, I also have loved you; Abide in My love.

John 17:23, ...And that the world may know that You have sent Me, and have loved them as You have loved Me.

Daniel 10:11, And he said to me, "O Daniel, man greatly loved, understand the words I speak unto you...

Ephesians 2:4, But God—so rich is He in His mercy! Because of and in order to satisfy the great, wonderful and intense love with which He loved us... (Amplified Version)

Ephesians 1:4, Just as He chose us in Him before the foundation of the world, that we should be holy and without blame before Him in love,

Hebrews 10:17, Then He adds, "Their sins and their lawless deed I will remember no more."

Ephesians 3:18-19, May be able to comprehend with all the saints what is the width and length and depth and height—to know the love of God which passes knowledge; that you may be filled with all the fullness of God.

Ephesians 2:1, And you He made alive, who were dead in trespasses and sins,

Ephesians 2:6-7, And raised us up together and made us sit together in the heavenly places in Christ Jesus, that in the ages to come He might show the exceeding riches of His grace in His kindness toward us in Christ Jesus.

2 Corinthians 5:21, For He made Him who knew no sin to be sin for us that we might become the righteousness of God in Him.

Lamentations 3:22-23, Through the Lord's mercies we are not consumed, because His compassions fail not. They are new every morning; Great is Your faithfulness.

1 John 3:1, Behold what manner of love the Father has bestowed on us, that we should be called the children of God.

Romans 8:31, What then shall we say to these things? If God is for us who can be against us?

Psalm 118:6, The Lord is on my side; I will not fear. What can man do to me?

Matthew 7:11, If you then, being evil, know how to give good gifts to your children, how much more will your Father who is in heaven give good things to those who ask Him!

Romans 8:37, Yet in all these things we are more than conquerors through Him who loved us.

1 John 4:16, And we have known and believed the love God has for us. God is love, and he who abides in love abides in God, and God in him.

Hebrews 4:16, Let us therefore come boldly to the throne of grace, that we may obtain mercy and find grace to help in time of need.

Psalm 145:9, The Lord is good to all, And His tender mercies are over all His works.

Song of Solomon 2:4, He brought me to the banqueting house, and His banner over me was love.

1 Timothy 1:14, And the grace…of our Lord… flowed out superabundantly and beyond measure for me, accompanied by faith and love… (Amplified Version)

APPENDIX

Amazing Love Ministries

Amazing Love Ministries (formerly Christian Faith Center) was established in 2001. We are a non denominational and bilingual church, part of the FCF fellowship of churches.

Our pastor's life changed in 1975 when as a young man he discovered John 14:12, indicating that the age of miracles and signs and wonders had never ceased.

Our vision is to proclaim the love and the goodness of God to a lost and dying world and equip the saints to do the works of Jesus.

Pastor Samuel Martinez was ordained in 1986. He teaches with humor and clarity the love of God, who we are in Christ Jesus and our authority as believers.

All contact information is listed here:

Email: Smartinez@cfaith.com

Correspondence:
Amazing Love Ministries
216 S. Citrus
P O Box 503
West Covina, CA 91791

About the Author

Samuel Martinez was ordained in 1986 and has been a full-time pastor since 2001. Prior to his work in the ministry, he served in the counseling field, with a master's degree in Marriage, Family and Child Counseling. Pastor Martinez's church offers both English and Spanish services, and his favorite themes to teach include the love and goodness of God. Pastor Martinez and his wife have been married over 45 years.

www.ingramcontent.com/pod-product-compliance
Lightning Source LLC
Chambersburg PA
CBHW071537080526
44588CB00011B/1701